Analytic Aesthetics
An Inquiry

New Writers imprint
The Natal Society Foundation
PIETERMARITZBURG
2011

Published by the Trustees of The Natal Society Foundation in 2011 as the first in its "New Writers" imprint. The imprint encourages non-fiction research and writing by young, previously unpublished, writers.

Natal Society Foundation website: http://natalia.org.za/
Author's e-mail address: thedisquisitionist@gmail.com

Editor: Peter Croeser
Design & layout: Jo Marwick

Body text and footnotes: Garamond

Illustrations:
Cover picture "Head & Shoulders" © Phila Mfundo Msimang 2011
Text illustrations © Phila Mfundo Msimang 2011

We acknowledge with grateful thanks permission to reproduce the poem "Opening the Cage: 14 Variations on 14 words" by the late Mr Edwin Morgan (1968) granted by the copyright administrators, Carcanet Press, Manchester, United Kingdom.

ISBN: 978-0-620-48343-8

For the "Love of Talking"

This is a book about philosophy,
Not an anthology of you and me:
It is to reinstate what seems now to be a separate part,
To re-establish the relationship between philosophy and its art.

~ Phila Mfundo Msimang

TABLE OF CONTENTS

If one is interested in the relations between fields which, according to customary academic divisions, belong to different departments, then he will not be welcomed as a builder of bridges, as he might have expected, but will rather be regarded by both sides as an outsider and troublesome intruder.

~ Rudolf Carnap (1963)

PUBLISHER'S PREFACE

Founded in Pietermaritzburg in 1851, the Natal Society has served the scientific and literary interests of the community of KwaZulu Natal, South Africa, for the past 160 years. It founded the city's Natal Museum (now a leading national institution) and the Natal Society Library. The latter was the largest privately-owned public library system in the country until its transfer to the Msunduzi Municipality in 2004, when it was renamed the Bessie Head Library.

Today the Natal Society Foundation continues the original aims of the Society "the general encouragement of habits of study, investigation and research" by funding scholarship, maintaining a specialist reference library, and publishing the journal Natalia. Recently the entire contents of the journal have been digitized and made freely available on its website.

This book introduces The Natal Society Foundation's "New Writers" imprint. The imprint encourages non-fiction research and writing by young, previously unpublished, writers. It complements its "Occasional Publications" imprint reserved for work of high academic merit but considered unviable by commercial publishers.

I am grateful to the following professors of the University of KwaZulu-Natal for reading an early draft of the manuscript: David Spurrett (Professor of Philosophy in the School of Philosophy and Ethics), Mbongeni Malaba (Professor and Head of English Studies), and Bill Guest (Professor Emeritus in Historical Studies).

The author of *Analytic aesthetics: an inquiry*, a philosophical discourse on communication theory, is Phila Mfundo Msimang, a young writer from Caluza, outside Pietermaritzburg.

The author's interest in the philosophy of communication started while he was still at school. He had become increasingly aware that many problems in society stem from poor communication.

During several years of intensive investigation, made possible by the vast resources of digitized academic books and research papers available through the internet, he began formulating his own ideas and conclusions. They resulted in the present book which he began writing shortly after turning 18.

The author addresses key areas in communication theory in the form of discussions and analyses of the philosophical principles involved, using his own poetry and a word picture to illustrate his arguments.

The book is unconventional, as is sometimes the author's use of diction. Not because he is unaware of the conventional terms employed in communication theory, but because of their limitations in addressing the issues that concern him. In some instances he has adapted or redefined terms. In others he introduces new terms to suit his purpose.

> "It is not our business to set up prohibitions, but to arrive at conventions".
>
> ~ Rudolf Carnap

Peter Croeser
Chairman, The Natal Society Foundation

AUTHOR'S PREFACE

But if there was one great insight in pragmatism, it was the insistence that what has weight in our lives should also have weight in philosophy.

~ Hilary Putnam (1999)

Whatever we conceptualise is philosophy and however it is expressed is an art. The purpose of this book is to introduce a familiar subject in a different light; primarily to show that all is of philosophy, and that no part of our lives can be divorced from it. It is for this reason that part of my life is also found here. But the book is not about my life, it is about philosophy; in particular, the underlying principles of communication.

While this book can be said to be about philosophy, I am not comfortable with calling myself a philosopher. There is a certain mysticism, even mystique, that I believe taints the definitions of philosophy and philosopher. For this reason I would prefer to call my inquiry disquisition, the setting out of the results of a formal inquiry; and myself a disquisitionist, an inquirer. Nonetheless philosophy itself is a recognised discipline, and for the sake of convention I have used the term in this book.

The Prelude discusses the importance of content and context, and their relationship. It is followed by three sections that I have called 'movements'. The movements illustrate the conjecture in different ways, emphasising different aspects of it. Poetry is the subject of the First Movement explicating the import of context in communication. The Second Movement serves as an interlude between the poetry of the First Movement and the word-picture of the Third Movement, in which the place of content is emphasised. The Third Movement is an illustrative analogue of an aspect of the communication of persons. Each is interdependent in that none of the three movements on their own are a complete illustration of the underlying principles of communication. In the last part of the book the Praxi serve the function of making explicit some of the most salient postulates, and their ramifications, that arise from the Prelude and the three movements.

I would like to thank my friends and family (the tribe as a whole) who have tolerated me. A special thanks goes to the publishers, The Natal Society Foundation, and their chairperson and editor on this project, Peter Croeser, without whose encouragement and support this book would not have materialised, but would have remained scattered papers beneath my bed. I would also like to thank Michael Pitchford of the University of KwaZulu Natal, Pietermaritzburg, for his early encouragement and discussions in philosophy. I would also like to extend my gratitude to Therese (Tessa) Dewhurst of the University of Cape Town, South Africa, for providing me with a paper I had requested from her, and Alice Crary of Lang College, New York, for sending me her book.

This study would not have been possible without open access through the internet to many of the books and papers consulted.

P. M. M.

PRELUDE

In which we re-evaluate the position of art and writing in philosophical discourse. We are introduced to the importance of both context and content, and their relationship which we are to grasp sufficiently in order to communicate with one another.

A rt, as the representation of things that are and that are not, is an invaluable way in which we communicate ideas. But art is more than things to which we believe need an audience. Art is expression. An expression is something born from an impression or an idea, which is then acted upon. Art is, after all, the manifestation of concepts in form. Art is anything that can be proposed. In other words, everything conceived of that is then expressed in any particular way is an art. [1]

In current philosophical discourse, there has been great neglect as to the substance of what has conventionally been known as art. The subject of this has been left to the 'philosophers of art' to explore. The ramifications of artistic works are seldom seen as a topic fit to be dealt with within the schools of philosophy proper although a great deal of philosophizing may go on, most notably about the definition of art. [2]

---

1   Thought and reflection are thus still a part of 'art' as they are acted upon in the mind (brain).
2   Kristin Hrehor (2007)

The substance of the arts has been dismissed to the province of art critics, as has that of the novel to literary critics. On inspection, however, one will find that even poetry or fiction, however rich and conceptually loaded it may be, will demand coherence within its own world. There is always a logic, a structure in which even a fiction is ordered. Whatever falls in the domain of concepts is in the scope of philosophy, and its mode an art.

Art, performed or otherwise, is a communication of functions both aesthetic and analytic. In communication we can call the former style, and the latter content. Style is not of its own but needs content, the material to be presented. Content is not a means of its own. It is senseless without context, without function, without structure. The core components of communication are the context which defines the rules and possibilities of engagement, the content which is the expression of concepts, the articulant who has made the expression or articulation, and the recipient who interprets the expression. The relation of these components to one another is the gist of communication, and it is this fundamental that this work attempts to explore.[3]

There is no expression without content. But content is just an expression's substance; be it words, gestures, music, pictures, other artefacts, or the like. Content is what is shaped and created through impression resulting in concepts, made manifest by expression. What gives meaning to content is form; namely the arrangement of its symbolism, and the cultural climate and ecology of those symbols. In short, what we probe is the context. Since context gives content meaning, it allows the broad symbolism of the content to be reduced to a specific sign as a negotiated symbol. The sign is a formal convention, or consensus. That is the aim of

---

3   Other entities may be said to 'communicate', and an individual may be said to communicate with himself; but, although the same rules generally apply, the focus of this work is on what makes the communication between persons possible.

what content should become in an expression so that it may be understood in its fullest and most proper sense.

It is inherent in an expression that it mean *something*. In the main, it is because it is an expression of a process or a thought. It is enough that something be expressed for it to be significant, since expression is consequential.[4] It is derived from antecedent impressions and results in particular ideas. A recipient, being the interpreter of an expression, cannot help but be affected by the expression just by virtue of recipientship. The expression is a form of stimulus and so, as a result, elicits a response.[5] How significant the meaning of a particular expression is, and the response of the recipient to it, is another matter altogether decided by cognition. The expression could be something unintelligible to the recipient, or even be an articulation the recipient experiences sub-consciously.

To an individual who may not understand Hebrew, and who may not be able to himself decipher the texts written in that language, content that arrives to him in Hebrew is communicatively ineffective. On the other hand, if the resources of speech, body language, tone, and gesture were available, other routes to approximate the sense of the articulation are open to him. For written content he can be aware of the text and its function as a text to communicate something, but the text means nothing in particular to him. The meaning of an expression outside of culture or convention is undecidable and can equally be interpreted with no conclusive justification for a particular interpretation the one way or the other.

---

4   Significance itself implies meaning, but this meaning should not be confused with what is meaningful within a particular discourse. Significance amounts to being noteworthy, but it is not necessarily meaningful in the communicative sense.

5   It is recognised that the process of articulation and interpretation is not exclusive and, in fact, can operate concurrently through mechanisms of feedback.

When culture or particular conventions are taken into account, however, then some phrases are more likely than others. For example "I do not eat pork" has a higher level of probability than "I take pleasure in eating pork" in Hebrew-speaking culture. Culture and convention place restriction on content into the constraints of that culture or convention.

Even within a language, individuals may be unable to understand one another because of their differences in expertise. Their diction may be exclusive to the respective guilds to which they belong, or it may be that the individuals may attach different meanings to the same words which they employ.[6] They derive different meanings or associations for their diction from their respective experiences.

The unique position of the individual in the communicative process necessitates that the individual's position be recognised as such: as subjective. What this means is that every expression that the individual articulates or interprets is subject to that individual's particular bias. This is not to be misunderstood to be a condition where bias makes the articulation and interpretation of expression a completely arbitrary or private affair where none can probe. Bias is the mechanism of relation. It relates expression to the personal experience and circumstance of the recipient or articulant respectively.[7]

The setting under which communication occurs includes the intended meanings from the articulator, the expression of the

---

6   John Locke (1690): "Their signification [is] perfectly arbitrary, [and] not the consequence of a natural connexion... They signify only men's peculiar ideas, and that by a perfect[ly] arbitrary imposition, [it] is evident, in that they often fail to excite in others (even that use the same language) the same ideas we take them to be signs of: and every man has so inviolable a liberty to make words stand for what ideas he pleases, that no one hath the power to make others have the same ideas in their minds that he has, when they use the same words that he does."

7   That is to say, bias justifies the subject "I".

content, and the interpretation of the recipient. Context is about the situation of what is expressed and how it is expressed which also includes the factors influencing the way in which individuals think about what is expressed. The context encompasses the unique situation of each individual involved, the cultures and experiences involved in the communication, and the possibilities and circumstance of their communication. Context is the totality of the factors of interaction. It is the basis of the inter-subjective nature of communication.

Although the fundamental context is the schema encapsulating communication between participants, and all the things which can be communicated between them, we can speak of particular contexts and context-bearers. Those would be perspectives within the greater context or schema. From these points of view are individuals actively involved in the inter-subjective process, where they bring together their biases through communication to meet each other in understanding. Where there is correspondence or congruence in their expressions, in the form and structure of their content, are there planes of discussion that can be explored meaningfully and reciprocally by the communicants in the exchange of expressions.

This book explores the relation between content and context, the role of the messenger (articulation), the role of the message in itself (content), the role of the recipient in interpretation (subjectivity), and the role of intention (function) from the messenger considered in terms of the message and its interpretation (inter-subjectivity).

Opening the Cage: 14 Variations on 14 words

I have nothing to say and I am saying it and that is poetry.
John Cage

I have to say poetry and that is nothing and I am saying it
I am and I have poetry to say and that is nothing saying it
I am nothing and I have poetry to say and that is saying it
I that am saying poetry have nothing and it is I and to say
And I say that I am to have poetry and saying it is nothing
I am poetry and nothing and saying it is to say that I have
To have nothing is poetry and I am saying that and I say it
Poetry is saying I have nothing and I am to say that and it
Saying nothing I am poetry and I have to say that and it is
It is and I am and I have poetry saying say that to nothing
It is saying poetry to nothing and I say I have and am that
Poetry is saying I have it and I am nothing and to say that
And that nothing is poetry I am saying and I have to say it
Saying poetry is nothing and to that I say I am and have it

~ Edwin Morgan (1968).

FIRST MOVEMENT:

The word as poetry

In which we see that for communication to be effective between individuals, they must share the necessary meanings of experience to understand the words and phrases they articulate to one another. Also, the basis of communication in context and its import in writing is here discussed, and how we manipulate the said context to serve our own purposes.

There is an apparent restriction in a book demonstrating a theory of communication. Writing is unable to exploit the full range of devices of articulation and expression available to individuals when communicating face-to-face.[8] In conversation one can draw on resources such as gesture, behaviour, interaction, locution, and inflexion. But these are unavailable to the writer who is completely dependent on his work to communicate meaning.

Likewise, the reader suffers the same limitation as the author.[9] At its most basic level, communication is a physical impression derived from the senses. Recognition of these impressions,

---

8   Giles Gray & Claude Wise (1959); Stewart Tubbs & Sylvia Moss (1987).
9   That one cannot converse with, or obtain feed-back from, a book or a television set is inconsequential to the fact that communication has taken place: i.e., a message has been articulated and interpreted. Reciprocity and feed-back are a function of conversation between communicants, and thus a higher consideration in communication.

whether word, gesture, or behaviour, is interpreted symbolically. Sign is the refinement of symbolism, the creation of necessary relations between the meanings assigned to symbols. Symbols, and their refinement in sign, are abstract; but are derived and implied from physical experience.[10] Communication in its fullest sense is an exchange of expression – a stimulation of meanings. Writing is then not only a manner of communicating, but it is also a model of communication.

The apparent limitation of writing is a fundamental parameter of this model. It limits the meanings dealt with to only those which are written (namely, the symbolic expression of meaning in written form). All other meanings derived are from direct experience.[11] It is even the case in the communication of novel ideas. The creation of a new concept is derived from the unique combination of familiar meanings already at the disposal of the individual. That an idea is new can only be concluded against the background of one's own experience. The understanding of novel concepts relies on having the necessary experience as a resource to draw on. New ideas are derived from, communicated, and interpreted or understood, through experience. In writing, this manipulation of meanings, the creation of novel concepts, is achieved through words and phrases which, it is assumed, are already familiar and understood.[12]

---

10 In other words, the fundamental assumptions of logic are empirical and are subject to empirical revision. Metalanguages, or higher levels of abstraction, are only implicitly subject to such verification. See Rudolf Carnap (1955).

11 The author is limited in communication to the meanings which he writes in the text, despite all of his own experiences which may have engendered the written text. The reader interprets the text through his own experience, but is restricted to the meanings which he can derive from the text. The only meanings to be dealt with are from the text.

12 For meanings which are not assumed it is customary that definitions, or citations, are given that employ basic or familiar concepts assumed to be part of the individual's experience resource base. See also Bertrand Russell (1913).

It does not follow that all meanings, and their manipulation, are legitimate.[13] Within the fundamental parameter of our model, namely that we are concerned only with symbolic meanings, we need rules that restrict the meanings used to those that are necessarily related to each other. The context must be refined to leave only those meanings that are necessary to the discourse in order to retain clarity of communication on its subject.

Imperative to the context of the discourse is the setting out of the relevant parameters which encompass all the necessary meanings; not the setting out of all those possible meanings. Constructions based on the experiences and situation of the reader superimposed for commonality with those of the author are too simplistic. They are out of focus and risk missing the point completely. The situation and conditions in which one may read or write are of a marginal utility in informing the refinement of context. Although it may seem as if the increase of precise detail creates the proper context, such detail may be superfluous.

The definition of relevancy in the formulation of parameters entails how (and how far) the context is to be refined. In an 'open' context everything is implied; but when the subject or mode is identified, only particular meanings retain relevance. The expressed meanings of the content retain their relevance by their necessity to the subject.

Other expressions peripheral to the subject are contingent on the fundamental parameter and are thus of limited, if any, relevance to the subject of discourse. Take, for example, an analysis of the performance of an automobile: the question of its locomotive force is imperative and necessary to the subject whereas considerations such as the colour of the automobile are inconsequential to the subject, even if contingent to the automobile. The reduction of

---

13   Legitimacy is a function of context.

9

expressions to necessary and contingent in relation to a particular subject refines the context to its proper range and limits, and sets the parameters to which all meanings should conform within the discourse.

Likewise with poetry. Understanding poetry is dependent on the context of the poem. Its fundamental constraint is within tradition, from whence all denominations of poetry are derived. Poetic expression is, *de facto*, bound by and bound within this context. But, as argued above, it is in the weighing of the subject, poetry or the subject of its poems in this particular case, which places the content of the form within its context of appropriate meanings.

The meanings of poetry stereotypically exploit the common meanings of words and concepts for general appeal. This usually sees poetic expression lag behind contemporary thought on special topics and scientific matters.[14] On this matter some commentators have gone as far as to say that "as science makes progress in any subject-matter, poetry recedes from it"[15] and that "the two cannot stand together... [as they are] two modes of viewing things which are contradictory of each other".[16]

The force of poetry has traditionally been emphasised to be in its form – in its style and affect, the aesthetic component. In other words, the manner of presentation has been taken to be of prime importance; with content, the analytic component, a secondary consideration on its affectual effectiveness.[17] It is enough that, in this conception of poetry, a poem be moving; the 'how' and 'why' of it are seen as superfluous, if not frivolous (although the affectiveness is created by the 'how' and 'what' of it).

---

14   Thomas Peacock (1820).
15   John Newman (1858).
16   *Ibid*
17   Percy Shelley (1840).

Such contingencies emphasised within the meaning of a work are manifestations of the affective fallacy.[18] There has to be in poetry a more sophisticated substance than emotional force and representational appeal for it to be significantly informative to the theory of communication, and not itself a rudimentary play of words as interjections or purely emotive expression. There must be an analytic aesthetic to reconcile the art of communication.

Nonetheless since style and affect are composed of content, and content within a context is meaningful, poetry can be analysed on its value in expression. In the same breath it is understood that what is a necessary feature in poetry may be scientifically contingent.[19] But this fact is only a result of how the parameters are set, i.e.: as a result of context.

In this movement the aim is to explicate the weight of context through poetry.

---

18   William Wimsatt & Monroe Beardsley (1949).
19   Paul Cantor (2004).

Lost

I once thought I was lost in myself
Only to find that I was someone else.
Trapped in the walls of depression,
I was a prisoner with no freedom.
Controlled by some other being being me,
Only as if I was not doing a good enough job
Of being myself.

This poem was written in 2005 and marks the beginning of a not very well remembered but adverse two and a half years.

In retrospect, those years were my first of disillusionment with the world, and periodic disenchantment with people. They were a prerequisite for my journey in philosophy.

> We cannot go beyond it [the philosophy] because we have not gone beyond the circumstances which engendered

it. Our thoughts, whatever they may be, can be formed only upon this humus; they must be contained within the framework which it [history] furnishes for them or be lost in the void or retrogress.

~ Jean-Paul Sartre (1960)

If we can be honest about love

In time I have come to know
That this life is more.
That this life is full of beauty;
A trait not uniquely your own.

Once, having been content with no one special,
There cannot exist a single everything.
You are not the world, you are not my philosophy.
How I wish you were, but my passions do not make true.
All I can hope is that you may walk this path with me.
May you see the significance in that?

This may not look like your common love-letter.
That is because this is more sincere
Than any such letters could ever wish to be.

I love you,
But never mind.

Love, as with any of the passions, is an irrationality in the sense that it affects the faculty of reason in such a way as to shift the focus and operation of the mind away from its usual state. Within the context of 'being in love' there are different rules and functions of priority operating in the mind.

St. Gregory the Great

Change the batteries in St. Gregory's halo!
Paint over her horns of phosphorescence!
Bleach back her wings of black,
And no good virtue must she lack!

Not a flaw,
Nor any imperfections.
I want the world to see
All the beauty she has given me.

Because I love her,
Because she is a hero:
Let no one see her in the light –
Amok.

This is a poem I wrote to my older brother, Lunga, for him and our younger sister, Lindelwa, about our grandmother, Leah Msimang. Whilst growing up, an aunt dubbed grandmother the 'female father'. This was because she had been the sole provider for her daughter, our mother, Lindiwe, and had provided refuge for us before and after the death of our mother. Her refuge, and in fact our own, was Florah "Aunti" Ziqubu (Majozi) who lived with us in Caluza for over 22 years until her death in 2011. I named Leah

17

St. Gregory the Great as she was indeed the female 'father', seen as a saint by all who know her.

The poem is about denial, hers and our own, about people and especially about each other. It is a poem dealing with the period in which Greg was doing volunteer work as a social worker for Project Accept, providing counselling and testing for HIV/AIDS. Her mission was to help those infected and affected by HIV/AIDS find closure so that she too could find closure on the circumstances around her daughter's death. She was trying to make right what only we knew were her wrongs, and it was seen as something done out of selflessness and sorrow. In the household we all knew, but never mentioned, that her philanthropy was driven by regret and remorse.

The poem *St. Gregory the Great* is about Gregory on the one hand, and about her humanity on the other.

A "Wish" in the vernacular

I once saved the man
who murdered me.
And now when there is
a sound in the darkness
which I cannot see,
there is nothing
I am more afraid of
than he
to, yet again,
call on me.

A memory reflected in this poem is of the circumstances around
my being stabbed outside my home in Caluza at the age of 14.

> They ask us why we mutilate each other like we do,
> and wonder why we hold such little worth for human
> life... But to ask us why we turn from bad to worse is
> to ignore from which we came. You see, you wouldn't
> ask why the rose that grew from the concrete had
> damaged petals. On the contrary, we would all celebrate

its tenacity; we would all love its will to reach the sun. Well; we are the roses, this is the concrete, and these are my damaged petals.

~ Tupac Shakur (2003)

We, the living

Life is nature's sarcastic spell,
Where what has not been designed ends just as well.
The joys that are experienced throughout this life
Define the disparities of strife.
From what sort of enigmatic solution
Comes forth this chaos, this confusion?

The gifts of a God.
What craft! What skill!
The great beast's most efficient art is to kill.
But this beast is special – it has the freedom of will?

Is there any duty to do?
Only that there is me because of you.
"So, where is it that we are going?"
The specious; not knowing.

Bones have been dug out of the deep
For man cannot yet find his sleep.
But can we not yet see,
That the universe is indifferent to a thing called 'me'?
Neither we, the living.

The poem is on the human condition. There is the question of community and the necessity of co-operation for survival.[20] It alludes to questions about whether or not we have already exceeded our marginal utility, and whether or not humanity is beyond the carrying capacity of the environment.[21] The poem suggests that if we do not find a sustainable equilibrium in which we are in

---

20   John Donne (1624)
21   Thomas Malthus (1826)

relative adherence to nature, working with it rather than working against it, the inevitable will come sooner rather than later: we could be manufacturing the eleventh hour of our existence.

> We live at a particularly perilous moment, one in which self-deception is a subject of increasing urgency. The planet itself faces a threat unknown in other times: its utter destruction [of life]. Whether that death be the quick one, from nuclear war and the catastrophic changes that would follow, or the slow ecological one, from the exorable destruction of forests and arable land and usable water, the human capacity for self-deception will have played its part.
>
> ~ Daniel Goleman (1985)

Blue grass, green skies

The roses wither away on the blue grass,
Not noticed by the people who pass.
The sun sets on this canvas of green sky,
Beauty I see, as on my head I lie.
The evening breeze whistles in my ears.
It brings with it these petals, the Earth's tears.
The sun sheds its last light,
But here I will sit out this night,
On blue grass, under green skies.

This poem is about a state of altered consciousness I experienced on the streets one night. It brings into question perception in general. Does any object truly have qualitative properties like a taste, feel, or definite colour? Is not the *game* of perception a question of reference?

It is evident from what we have found, that there is no colour which preeminently appears to be the colour of

23

the table, or even of any one particular part of the table — it appears to be of different colours from different points of view, and there is no reason for regarding some of these as more really its colour than others.

~ Bertrand Russell (1912)

Senses

When you were motionless,
I felt your shiver.
Seemingly odourless,
I smelt your fear.
You were not crying,
but I taste your tear.

I have seen you
in this darkness;
in your silence,
I heard you come by.

I feel no soul independent
of another, nor the senses.

What is the soul and what could its function possibly be? Is not
the introduction of the soul *ad hoc*? Is the concept of the soul not
redundant?

> The mind-body problem can be posed sensibly only so
> far as we have a definite conception of body. If we have
> no such definite and fixed conception, we cannot ask
> whether some phenomena fall beyond its range.
>
> ~ Noam Chomsky (1987)

Smoking time; pipe of thoughts

Fly he does, in his own time,
To places he finds secretly sublime.
Of him it is only fair to say;
As bright as a time of the day,
As dark as the shadow he scatters,
Impatient are his logic & love: incommensurable matters.
And having them equally divide his head and his heart,
Time threatens that one he may lose, the other to part.
"But be silent for me" he may say
As he listens to nature lecture away.
His only accomplice being his vice,
This is his meditation's price.

But still, on the ceilings he sits,
Waits and wonders.
Loading his pipe;
Smoking time.

This poem is about the dichotomy between the intuitions and reason. It highlights that what matters in philosophy is the substance put forth to be evaluated; not the special case one may build around it. Of the philosopher's circumstance and that reflected in his times, all that is considered is what is necessary and consequential to his subject. All else is fundamentally of a historic curiosity.

Philosophy is not the owl of Minerva that takes flight after history has been realized in order to celebrate its happy ending; rather, philosophy is subjective proposition, desire, and praxis that are applied to the event.

~ Michael Hardt and Antonio Negri (2000)

SECOND MOVEMENT:

The word as substance

*In which we see the importance of content in a message and the
role of the articulant as context-bearer or agent, whose providing
of context makes the message intelligible. We see that the context
is only useful so far as there is content to fulfil it.*

Words are functions in themselves in that they remain
meaningful even when in isolation from other words
(i.e., when accompanied by an explanatory action),
and are functions of each other in the sense that the combination
and manipulation of words is also meaningful in the construction
and communication of concepts.[22] How a word was originally
derived and used is within the subject of etymology. Its derivation
and use is an accident of biology and history – not an innate
property of the thing to which the word or concept refers.[23] The
representation could have taken any form.[24] Its meaning and
sense can change – they are part of an inter-related web of words

---

22   Gottlob Frege (1967); Umberto Eco (1976).

23   Benjamin Whorf (1950).

24   David Hume (1739): "We may change the names of things, but their
nature and their operation on the understanding never change". Such
a statement needs to be qualified. The complexity of a term, and the
associative effectiveness of a term, has direct bearing on how a term is
lodged in memory, hence also how that concept will be recalled. Thus, a
change in denotation can be sufficient in altering the recollection, and, as
a result, the understanding, of a particular concept (through, for example,
a change in association).

and phrases that are a response to the influences of the time, the *zeitgeist*.[25] The thing to which the word or concept refers is subjectively assigned to the stimulus.[26]

All meaningful expressions have rules and constraints determining their relations however it is that these expressions are constructed (formally or otherwise). It is in this sense that expressions cannot be free. The meaning of an expression is inherent in the context of the content.

If an expression can be made without a context, it is meaningless. But what expression could possibly be made without a context, or how could one possibly express the meaningless? There are things we intend to be meaningless and they can only be understood as such because of the recognition of the author or artist's intent, not because those expressions in themselves do not mean anything. We can only deduce intention from the author's expressions – from the content in question. As for example, a negative definition or negation of a meaning (like the word 'nothing', or concepts of 'not' or 'emptiness' in general) can be used as device to state a 'meaninglessness' or a deficiency in particular meanings although these, themselves, are meanings.[27]

The context of an expression is held within the very expression itself, but intent seems to be more elusive. But intent can be ascertained through knowledge of why an expression was made, namely 'to what ends'. It is often said that it is the intent of what one is expressing that determines the meaning of the expression

---

25 Stewart Tubbs & Sylvia Moss (1987) p. 115: "We can qualify the Sapir-Whorf hypothesis by saying that as a person learns the language of a given culture or subculture, his or her attention is directed towards aspects of reality or relationships that are important to that context...".

26 Giles Gray & Claude Wise (1959) p. 485: "*The meaning itself is a faculty of the relation between the symbol and the datum of experience*" (original emphasis).

27 Words used as device take the role of functors, or function words, whose meanings are then logically connective. See Rudolf Carnap (1937).

received, and not what one is literally expressing. This is most misleading. This view assumes that one could know what another individual means before, and even regardless of, what it is that is said or expressed – regardless of the content.

But what is said or expressed is always significant to the meaning conveyed because the meaning is relative to it, as even intent is expressed through content. This still stands in contexts of deception.[28] But intention may be misunderstood because of unfamiliarity with the form in which the expression comes (as, for example, an archaic phrase). Equally, orthodox modes of expression could be misleading because of communicative incompetence (since communicating is a skill requiring competence in its various modes of articulation and interpretation).[29] Evaluation can only be made through content although content, itself, is defined by the context.

The rules of expressive communications are externally negotiated, and the employment of any language is in relation to the rules and regulations of that language.

The view of any particular thing will always be skewed by convention, as convention is a common context. When ideas cannot be expressed clearly within a convention, a new schema must be set to be followed by those who are to understand what is said or done within it. Failing which, the intention of the author must be aligned to the prevailing conventions if the intended meaning of the expression is to be understood as it is (or as it was meant).

The expression between persons is, therefore, also inextricably linked to intention; firstly because intention gives rise to an

---

28 Tessa Dewhurst (2009).
29 Justin Kruger & David Dunning (1999).

expression and, secondly, because it informs the context in which the meaning of the expression is to be concluded. What an expression was 'made for' is an indication of what it is, or what it is meant, to mean. Unfamiliarity with a convention results in failure to comprehend expressions in that form. For example, the meaning of the following may seem incomprehensible:

KDFDG
ACBDC
FORQE
TPMI
PMOY

or: uidfuhdi"kjcxnv!k]ho/#cknq2klmn9ὠonme--fjimcokcn.

But these examples may be sensible under a number of interpretations, e.g.: as a schematic, another type of code, or a postmodernist interpretation (in which case it could be abstract, counter-intuitive, or 'meaningless'). The context is inherent in the expression, but the meaning of the form is hard to deduce since the intent of the expression is not at all clear and neither is there content to deduce the context from. Only the constraints essential to the form are explicit. The definition or refinement of the context, encompassing the content that could be expressed within it, is unresolved. The meaning of the form is open to any interpretation within the context. Form is given an emphasis here which makes it as exhaustible as the context itself.

It is thereby ambiguous within that framework. Such can be the ambiguity of unclear or varying definitions that we find in non-formalized systems like natural language.[30] Alternatively, there is formal ambiguity or undecidability if all relations are formally defined as in logic or mathematics. (Take, for example, the 19th century German mathematician David Hilbert's 1st, 2nd, and 10th problems dealing with mathematical undecidability.)[31]

---

30   Keith Devlin (2006).
31   David Hilbert (1902); Solomon Feferman (1998).

The primacy of the fundamental context must always be observed in the analysis of content; and the weight of intent within expression must always be taken into account where it is present (and it is always present in the communication of persons), because it is the point of reference from which the meaning is to be deduced. The entire substance of expression is found in content, and the refinement of context that engenders the meanings of this content is found from the subject of the content itself. The relationship between content and subject is analytic as the meanings of content are circular to the refined context,[32] although even these meanings are of combinations derivative of experience.

When the context implies intentionality or agentry, then the communication of persons is involved. The meaning of the expressions will reflect this fact as they are reflexive of the articulant or agent. The agentry tempers how the relations amongst the objects or phenomena will be perceived by the agent itself, and also how this information will be relayed by the agent.

The deduced meaning of the world will follow the mode of the agent because the agent is the interpreter, the context-bearer. The world must be seen through the agent's perspective if others are to reach an understanding of the agent or its expressions. This is to say that the context of the agent must be weighed against the substance the agent presents in order to achieve an understanding of its expressions; but also that understanding is dependent on familiarity with the content with which the agent is concerned. Content can never be divorced from the matter and is, in fact, imperative to it.[33]

---

32 Willard Quine (1951).
33 A meaningful generalization or context is always in reference to instances of its application, to content.

To say, therefore, that thought cannot happen in an instant, but requires a time, is but another way of saying that every thought must be interpreted in another, or that all thought is in signs.

~ Charles Peirce (1868)

THIRD MOVEMENT:

The word as image

*In which we analyse the import of context and content in a word
picture to illustrate that the context of expressions not only gives
expression significance, but is also responsible for what meanings
are attributed to particular expressions. We judge the merits of
the facts contained in the expression, and how these facts measure
against the context in which they are presented.*

The word picture overleaf is made of various textual
components that create the pictorial devices in the work.
The pictorial imagery (the image which we get from the
shapes and figures – the pictorial component) is that of a couple
on a picnic one sunny day. In contrast, the textual imagery (the
image which we get from the meaning of the text – the textual
component) is of a couple conversing at night. The pictorial
component stands in contrast to the textual component, giving
a different frame of interaction to that of the pictorial devices
alone. Taken in conjunction with the meaning of the textual
components which compose these pictorial devices, we find that
the interaction between the imagery is metaphor or that it produces
its own extended meaning. Together, these two components say
something other than what each would individually. It is the
fusion of the textual component and the pictorial component
that create a combined imagery that we can call, quite simply, the
hybrid image. It is within the hybrid image that the actual meaning
of the communication is found.

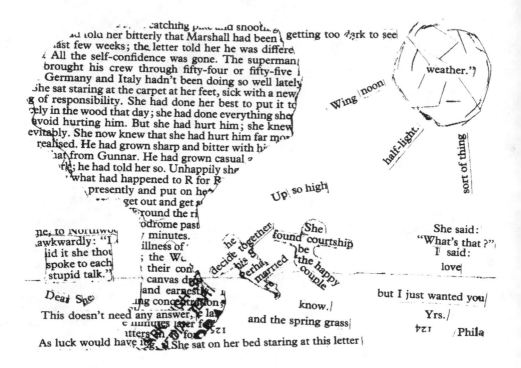

catching pine and smooth ...
...d told her bitterly that Marshall had been getting too dark to see
...ast few weeks; the letter told her he was differe...
... All the self-confidence was gone. The superman
brought his crew through fifty-four or fifty-five
Germany and Italy hadn't been doing so well lately
She sat staring at the carpet at her feet, sick with a new
g of responsibility. She had done her best to put it to
cly in the wood that day; she had done everything she
avoid hurting him. But she had hurt him; she knew
evitably. She now knew that she had hurt him far mo...
realised. He had grown sharp and bitter with hi...
...at from Gunnar. He had grown casual ...
...; he had told her so. Unhappily sh...
...what had happened to R for R
...presently and put on he...
...get out and get ...
...round the ri...
...odrome past

Wing noon
half-light
weather."
sort of thing

Up so high

ne, to Northwo...
...awkwardly: "I...
...id it she thou...
...spoke to each...
...stupid talk."

he decide together
his
perha married
She found courtship
be the happy
couple

illness of
; the We
t their con...
canvas d...
and earnest...
...ing concentration;

Dear She
This doesn't need any answer, e la...
c minutes later f...
...tters on to for...

know.

and the spring grass

She said:
"What's that?"
I said:
love

but I just wanted you

Yrs.

124 Phila

As luck would have it, ... She sat on her bed staring at this letter

The "Pastoral Piece" is adapted from "19 Baker Road's Pastoral Piece", a word picture created by the author in 2009. As a complete work, "19 Baker Road's Pastoral Piece", is made up of text fragments selected from Nevil Shute's novel "Pastoral" (1944) mounted on board, and framed with planks held together by hand-cut copper strips.

On the source of illumination

The element in the top-right corner of the work is a pictorial representation of the sun. The shape and orientation of this element suggests this strongly. Even if we look at the textual component *weather"* at the element's centre, the pictorial imagery suggests that the

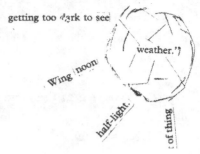

textual component *"weather"* is an allusion to 'sun' and hence a label of the element in question.

But taken together in context, the textual components that generate the pictorial device create a contrary image; namely, one of the late evening or night where the sun cannot be said to be present as depicted by the pictorial imagery. The textual components that create the pictorial device of the radial arms of the Source of Illumination are made of the phrases: *"getting too dark to see"*, *"wing noon"*, *"half-light."*, *"sort of thong"*. As a whole, semantically, it is possible to make sense of the phrases as conveying a unified message. The nonsensical or otherwise ambiguous phrase *"wing noon"* is of obscure meaning. But just on reading or as is found in this particular context, it is apparent that the 'wing' in *"wing noon"* and the entire phrase, in fact, is not used in the common or conventionally grammatical sense. It is bordering absurdity. What type of "noon" is 'wing'?[34] But it is clear when we also look at the textual components *"half-light."* and *"sort of thong"* we can deduce that what appears to be the case pictorially is not, in fact, the case textually.

---

34 In English, when two words are put together, the first word serves as a classification or type of the second word which is the prime subject of the concept expressed in word. Therefore a "race-car" is 'a type of car', whereas a "car-race" is 'a type of racing'.

The phrase *"wing noon"* can be taken to mean 'something that is not quite noon' or could be extended further to mean 'something that is *not* noon at all'. In essence, we can be certain that it is not mid-day represented in this element as it is contrary to the full sense derived.

The pictorial device in the element suggests a bright sunny day whilst the textual components imply that there is no direct sunlight, and that the element cannot be the sun. That would leave the question, what is the meaning of the component *"weather"* in this broader context amongst the other elements in the figure. Even if we remain with the interpretation of the word 'weather' being a metaphor for the word 'sun', we would only have to extend the metaphor of this imagery to be that *"weather"* is not a label on the element, but that it represents a reflection of *"weather"* or 'the sun'. In effect, the two components (the textual imagery and pictorial imagery) combine to create the hybrid image of a full moon reflecting the light of the sun.

On agents and intention

Next, we will look at the two figures that represent a couple. The design of this pictorial device is almost unrealistic – the two figures have irregular postures and rigid frames with no detail (take, for example, the  fact that they have no fingers, nor hair, et cetera) that gives them the look of figurines or tin robots rather than that of people.[35] But this fact in no way stands out because the form is that of the entire work (ie: word picture). Deductively, if not intuitively, we assume that these figures *are* persons in the representational sense.

---

35   See Eric Joyner. *Tin Robots, Submerged* (2009).

The contrast of the pictorial device is only augmented by the textual components here, as the figures are given their identities and depth by the words which compose them. We can distinguish between the figures as one being male and the other being female since the first word in each respectively is *"he"* and *"she"*. These elements represent persons, so it is the figures that project themselves out into the world within the work. Accordingly, the textual components are anticipated by the sentiment and observation of the two pictorial figures. For example, in the element Source of Illumination the textual components are composed of phrases expressing opinion about the state of affairs within the world of the work. Every element is a projection from the agents *"he"* and *"she"*, and they are also projections of their own intent or function.

We see that the *"he"* figure is leaning back pointing at the textual component *"Up so high"*. This component is in an open area above the figures and is being pointed at by the *"he"* figure. Having this in mind, and having considered the meaning of the phrase 'Up so high', we can deduce that the component *"Up so high"* is reference to one thing or another 'up in the heavens' or 'up in the sky'. As we have established the fact that it is dark or that it is night time, one may assume that the elements of the component *"Up so high"* are the stars. Whatever it may be, the *"he"* figure is pointing at it.

The *"he"* figure is relaxed in posture and could be indulging in the casual activity of star-gazing (as opposed to studying the stars) or just looking out into the distance at something. As for the *"she"* figure, she does seem startled which we can see by the rigidness of her posture. The *"she"* figure is pointing out into the distance in front of her. From the orientation of the *"he"* figure, it seems as if he is unaffected as he is absorbed within his own doings or observations. The *"she"* figure is pointing at an element made out of a textual component that does not make a clear representation of a specific object in reality. This component reads: *"She said: "What's that?" I said: love".* This component shows that these figures are projecting themselves to even the abstract, as they too are in relation to them. Since both the *"he"* and *"she"* figures are the only recognisable agents in the piece, it is only rational to assume that such sentiment or dialogue was between them. They are the only components that are directive or projective in their elements, making them the agents of the work within the world of the work.

The rest of the textual components making up the *"he"* and *"she"* figures are stereotypical thoughts and intentions that are expected to be found in such a relationship. The figure *"he"* has the words *"he decide together his perhaps married"* which is in purported congruence to the *"she"* figure's elements *"She found courtship be the happy couple"*. Superficially, it seems as if the two figures are not of the same intentions because of their mannerisms but the intent drawn by the textual component shows that they are seemingly in concert.

Other elements reflective of the agents and intent

We had deduced above that the figures *"he"* and *"she"* project themselves out into all the elements of the work, having the textual component anticipated by the sentiment and observation of these two hybrid images. Under analysis, we see this in all the components: the Source of Illumination, as discussed, has the textual component composed of phrases expressing opinions about the state of affairs within the world of the work which, in turn with the meaning of the pictorial component, created the hybrid imagery of the pictorial and textual concepts as one. We concluded in saying that every element within the work is the projection of the agents *"he"* and *"she"*. The last three elements in the work, which I will discuss first together as a unit and then separately, are explicitly so.

The Tree, Pot-Plant, and Ground components have been less adapted than all the other elements in the work (i.e.: they are closer to being excerpts as these components are made of textual elements more intact than the rest of the components in the work with the exception of the Ground component which is selected in the same manner as the element the Source of Illumination). These components are all connected by Ground, so I will analyse their interaction as such. Understanding these components as the reflections or projections of the intent of the "*he*" and "*she*" figures, the elements making up the textual component are in no way obscure.

The Ground component is also of two parts as is to be expected: the pictorial imagery, being the ground, and the textual imagery, being an expression of emotion. The pictorial component of Ground is defined by a line on which things rest and protrude out of. The textual component of Ground is scattered within it, reading: *"Dear" "Sne" "This doesn't need an answer," "As luck would have it" "She sat on her bed staring at this letter" "and the spring grass" "know." "but I just wanted you" "Yrs." "124" "Phila".* Also important to note is that the orientation of the component Ground is beneath the figures "*he*" and "*she*", as it should be pictorially, but as a textual device it is pregnant with implication. Within the component Ground we find the hybrid image of the couple's hidden emotions. We see this through the textual component of Ground that conveys emotion and desire in conjunction with the pictorial device of Ground. It conveys those things that lie beneath the surface that are hidden – the emotions.

Looking at the Pot-Plant element we find the text *"me, to Nor*[...] *awkwardly: "I* [...]*id it she thou*[...] *spoke to each stupid talk."* within the pictorial device. First in analysing this component from the purely textual perspective, still as a projection of the two figures, it shows that they are using the phatic devices of language – in other words, just making 'small talk' or just chatting. These elements are on the Ground element; the component is above the surface. The metaphor used here is that of the figures' "*stupid talk*" to be what is apparent superficially; i.e.: above the surface or the Ground. Beneath the surface though, which is within the Ground element, is where we identify the deeper meaning of their "*stupid talk*". In other words, the hybrid imagery is of the couple's conversation seeming frivolous whereas, beneath the surface, we find that their conversation is more profound.

The Pot-Plant component is a pictorial representation of a pot-plant container. If we look at the function of a pot-plant container, it is an object in which plants (in this case, it is specifically referring to a tree because of the Tree component to follow) start their early development. Hence, the Pot-Plant component, in relation to these considerations, is the representation of something new, young, and perhaps even innocent.

It stands in contrast to the Tree component which represents what is older and more mature. The textual components in the Ground element communicate the intentions and wishes of the agents. The Tree element is partly within and partly without the Ground element, as would be the case of a tree growing out of the ground. If we are to re-relate this to the components, we could interpret them as that which grows from the intentions and emotions of the agents. It is something

catching pine and snootk .
.J told her bitterly that Marshall had been
last few weeks, the letter told her he was differe
All the self confidence was gone The superman
brought his crew through fifty four or fifty five
Germany and Italy hadn't been doing so well lately
She sat staring at the carpet at her feet, sick with a new
of responsibility She had done her best to put it to
ely in the wood that day, she had done everything she
avoid hurting him. But she had hurt him, she knew
evitably. She now knew that she had hurt him far mo
realised. He had grown sharp and bitter with bi
at from Gunnar He had grown casual
he had told her so Unhappily she
what had happened to R for P
presently and put on he
get out and get
round the ri
odrome past
minutes
illness of
the We
their con
canvas d
and earnest
ng congregation
d any answer, la
minutes later f
tters R fo
e i She

that matures and has a life-cycle; viz.: it is the Tree element that grows out of the Ground element that is, in fact, what has matured from the Pot-Plant element. All of which is from the projection of the agents.

The Tree element is composed of phrases like *"All the self-confidence was gone... avoid hurting him. But she hurt him; she knew... He had grown sharp and bitter... He had grown casual [...]; he had told her so. Unhappily sh[e]..."*, which communicates the future discord of the agents (if we are to look at the three elements as chronologically conjoined), or that the discord is inevitable from the elements of the component Ground on which it is based.

Summary

The *Pastoral Piece* is composed of textual components creating the pictorial devices which are not positively affirmed by the actual text that composes them. The exception is the two figures which are the agents of the work in the world of the work. This makes the elements in the work self-referential in that all are in relation to the agents. Yet the work did not synthesize its own meanings so there are no real agents within the work, and the self-referential and self-reflexive elements are only introduced by the level of interpretation of it.

Endnote

Within any discussion, there are things not explained but assumed to be self-explanatory or self-evident. There are explicit assumptions, for example, that we both understand the language in which we are communicating; and there are also implicit assumptions such as that we understand the concepts we are communicating to each other. But these foundations of discussion are not always as we would suppose them to be because they are not 'givens' (which is explicitly so in the former case, and implicit in the latter). The question is: what assumptions have been taken for granted here?

We could ask 'what is this abstraction?', the word-picture above.[36] Who is to say that it is even an abstraction? It could be sufficient to say that it is just an object of its own. After all, what evidence is there that it is anything other than just that – an object unrelated to any other?[37] This question may sound trivial but it is key to what gives us an understanding of things communicated; that we see relations between entities and processes. Thought and all concepts in communication are only through discrimination.[38]

What has bearing here is not only the relation of the concepts conveyed through the use of written language, but also that of its constituents. To follow the discussion you would have had to hypothesise and theorise the possibility that the constituents, the marks on the page, are more than just an arbitrary array of objects. To follow the argument one needs to perceive the objects as being rationally distributed, and to recognise them as symbols that are signs or simple representations of things (general symbolic expression). Thence to recognise that the symbolism is representational of concept – not object. That is to say that signs and symbols represent a concept about a thing, and not any thing itself. The actual thing is of its own.[39] The rules that govern the world of the abstract (i.e.: signs and symbols) do not govern the things they stand for, but concepts about them.[40]

---

36 Art? But art is the way in which any concept is expressed, so art is too general a category. Perhaps we could call it exhibitional art because the mode is made specifically for exhibition. It is the difference between the art of speech and the art of public speaking: it is a mode within a mode, a method of expressing within the general way of expression. It is an abstraction in the sense that it is *an* art.

37 Roman Ingarden (1964); Gilles Deleuze (1968). See also Michel Foucault (1969).

38 Andrey Vyshedskiy (2008).

39 It could be argued that marks on a page are also of their own, but this point is trivial since we have established their employment as symbols. The things these symbols represent may be theoretical or otherwise. Things may have a conceptual or a physical ontological status. Things are processes or objects, imaginary or actual.

40 Alfred Tarski (1944).

The individual must have recognised that the employment of these symbols implies the intersubjectivity of what they are to communicate; that the rules of a language are of an interdependent, mutually concluded, nature between the users of that language.

Without having theorised or hypothesised (to have discriminated) the object would remain an arbitrary entity and have no meaning beyond its literal recognition. For example: a coffee table is then just a table, or shaped wood, or just wood, or a thing of a particular shape; or, as a matter of fact, just a unique thing of itself. It is to say that every substant thing is of its own – without relation or equivalence – and unique in the sense that it is void of all category. This creates contradiction. Are there unique things, and are these not members of the group of unique things?[41] But the mind operates on relations and discrimination. The literal recognition of any one thing is immediately pregnant with association and prejudice.[42]

Within the pictorial imagery we find smaller juxtaposed images of a different mode, composed of smaller symbols (being the words and letters respectively). We recognise a divide between the 'word image' and the pictorial imagery of the words. They are separate and divided from each other by their difference in mode, which necessitates a difference in their levels of analysis.[43] Only

---

41 Bertrand Russell (1903).
42 David Hume (1748); Andrey Vyshedskiy (2008).
43 If we look at the work *The Treachery of Images (This is not a pipe)* (1929) by René Magritte, we find a similar scenario. An image (a painting of a pipe) is expressed within the same frame where a phrase (*"Ceci n'est pas une pipe"* – this is not a pipe) is also expressed, but the phrase is explicitly non-affirmative of the image. In fact, the words are the denial of the picture. But these two devices remain separate and cannot be stated in equivalence. The sentence cannot deny itself and the picture cannot deny itself, but in conjunction they can be used to purportedly create this contradiction. Further analysis would show, however, because of the separation of these devices, the picture and the words are incommensurable; thus they argue past each other. This is because they are not of the same level of analysis by virtue of their difference in symbolic representation in the attempt to

one element of the pictorial imagery is reaffirmed. The textual components of each element are not explicitly descriptive of any of the elements with the exception of the agents, the two figures of personage. At most, the textual component is a teleological description which not only implies the identity of the persons, but is also reflected in all the elements of the work, making it a self-referential feedback loop.[44] The affirmation allows the two 'human-like' figures to be the source and reference of the teleology, thereby allowing the world of the work to be of their own projection.

It is assumed that the work above is seen as an abstraction on two accounts: firstly as a symbolic expression of some type (more specifically, an art form) and, secondly, as a generic re-creation of the detail in *19 Baker Road's Pastoral Piece*. The work presents its abstractions in two main kinds as gathered from above. Namely: the pictorial imagery of the concepts stimulated by the shapes on the one hand, and the textual imagery of the concepts generated by the words and phrases in the work on the other. But their sense is completed by their hybridization. It is only through relation that the message is understood.

refer to the same thing. "This is not a pipe" is not a pipe but a sentence; and only if "That is not the symbolic representation of a pipe" were to replace the phrase would it serve as a paradox, but a similarly weak one at that. It is true that it is not a pipe but contradictory and false that it is not a representation of one.

44   See the discussion on Maurits Escher's *Drawing Hands* (lithograph, 1968) in Douglas Hofstadter (1999).

I wanted to write that my work consists of two parts: of the one which is here, and of everything which I have not written. And precisely this second part is the important one.

~ Ludwig Wittgenstein (1921)

PRAXI[45]

In which we recognise in: 1. there being a drive for language in its simplest sense; 2. that the consequence of the amended system of signs is the view that even if experience is private, language is not; 3. that language is a quasi-independent system of signs; 4. that the differences of mankind are not so great so as to bar communication as there is a common basis for all world views; 5. that understanding need not be a metaphysical concept, but an empirical one; 6. that all unknown words referring to meanings need to be learnt for their meanings in order to be known; 7. that there are degrees of analysis within the system of signs; 8. that when the system works ideally there is a full disclosure of the necessary information; 9. that the message is to be taken on its own merits.

1. Ideology as incentive

1.1 The supremacy of philosophy over our activity is self-evident.[46] There is nothing that can be conceived of that is not in the scope of philosophy, and nothing that we consciously pursue that is not driven by ideology.

Ideology is the ordering of meanings towards ends – the incentive, or motive force, behind our conceptualized

---

45 Aesthetically, I prefer the term "praxi" for the plural of the Greek πρᾶξη (praxis) over the commonly used "praxes" or the less common "praxii". Praxi is used here in the sense of 'the proper way of doing things'.

46 It is the determiner of our economics, law, politics, and the rest of the faculties of man including science – it is the sum of mankind's entire conceptual existence. See John Dewey (1938).

actions.[47] The meanings are collected and constructed from the result of impressions and experience manipulated by the machinery of the mind. Although ideology is derived from our biological imperatives,[48] its creation and application by the mind is invented and artificial,[49] as is apparent in language.

---

47   Abraham Maslow (1943).
48   Joseph Rhawn (2000): "Buried within the depths of the cerebrum are several large aggregates of limbic structures and nuclei which are preeminent in the control and mediation of memory, emotion, learning, dreaming, attention, and arousal, and the perception and expression of emotional, motivational, sexual, and social behavior including the formation of loving attachments. Indeed, the limbic system not only controls the capacity to experience love and sorrow, but it governs and monitors internal homeostasis and basic needs such as hunger and thirst".
49   Ernst Mayr (1974).

2. The use of sign

2.1 In a message a sign is the representation of a particular thing, the signified is that particular thing the sign represents, and the signifier is the attributor of the sign to that particular thing. What separates the sign from just a symbol, which is also a general representation or abstraction, is that the generalization is formally defined (by which we mean the definition of things by establishing necessary relations between them).[50]

The initial dependence of sign on the signified necessitates that we first make sense of the world through our 'biological language' and that this bank of perception, experience, and understanding is adapted towards the 'learnt language system'. Learnt language systems are languages dependent on intersubjective communication which organise and re-categorize information. This includes naturally evolved human languages (as well as constructed languages such as Esperanto), and formal languages (artificial languages such as those employed in mathematics, logic, or computer programming). Learnt language systems, however, are still subject to the scrutiny of the biological language system.

Impression and perception are what triggers the machinery. Stimuli elicit a response, and the cognition of the event is a stimulus in itself. It is thus a loop, a feed-back mechanism to cognition, regulating the relationship between both the biological language and the learnt language.[51]

2.2 The biological language system is based on the internal (biological) rules of the individual, and the learnt language system is based on principles outside the individual. The

---

50 These uses are not conventional. See Ferdinand de Saussure (1959).
51 Giles Gray & Claude Wise (1959); Stewart Tubbs & Sylvia Moss (1987).

individual is always subject to the intersubjectivity of the learnt languages, i.e.: the consensus on the use and meaning of terms by the community in which they are being employed. Expressiveness in the learnt language is only effective within the constraints of the biological language system. The learnt language can artificially transcended the communications of the biological language system, but remains a function of the biology that both engenders and deciphers it.[52]

The flexibility of the conceptual boundaries we see in language does not reflect a flexibility of the capacity of the mind which is fixed and cannot be transcended. We are limited in language, as in all things, by the nature of our biology.[53]

---

52   Alfred Ayer (1940).
53   Morten Christiansen & Nick Chater (2008).

3. Language as mirror

3.1 There can be no proposition without the possibility of its own negation.[54] That is a direct result of the structure of language and logic. Language mirrors itself.

3.2 There is currently a great occupation with the accident of language and the nature of word. In keeping with tradition, a perplexed and often contradictory 'word analysis' and diction is employed.[55] Adherents employ a semantics and etymology based on a metaphysics that claims that the haphazard facts of language are an accurate description of the sign and the signified. Even the human condition is often approached in terms of denomination (i.e., the labels to which people are designated).[56]

There is a misconception that the signified is made and properly defined by the signifier or sign itself. Whether tribal ritual, Plato's philosophy of essences, the human measure of Protagoras, the fallacy of etymological necessity, racialism, religious belief in the Word or Destiny, it is purported that the sign satisfies the signified. In other words, how a thing

---

54 Ludwig Wittgenstein (1921): "If we cannot speak of doubt we cannot speak of knowledge either. It makes no sense to speak of knowing something within a context of which we cannot possibly doubt it."

55 Arthur Schopenhauer (1851): "The result is, they put what they have to say into forced and involved language, create new words and prolix periods which go around the thought to cover it up. They hesitate between the two attempts of communicating the thoughts and of concealing them... This mask of unintelligibility holds out the longest; this only in Germany, however, where it was introduced by Fichte, perfected by Schelling, and attained its climax with Hegel, always with the happiest results. And yet nothing is easier than to write so that no one can understand; on the other hand, nothing is more difficult than to express learned ideas so that everyone must understand them."

56 Mogobe Ramose (2003).

is designated is purportedly sufficient to describe all the conditions of the thing whereas the thing's characteristics hold true no matter how the thing, and what of the thing, is signified. The assumption that the sign or symbol necessarily denotes the signified, and exhaustively so, does not take into account that the agent of signification (the signifier) does so at his or her own convenience.

The sign is a formalized relation and, therefore, does not mirror reality necessarily.[57]

3.3 The deconstruction of concepts is the dissection and examination of the basis of ideas. In deconstruction we sometimes find that novel concepts are introduced, derived from outside the particular context, which then bring contradiction and controversy.[58] If operating within a specified context, the involvement of the surrounding ecology of contexts requires that the relations must be made clear so as to be refined to an analogous plane (i.e., to have the concepts analysed at an equivalent level of analysis in order to stay true to their operational meanings).[59] As with the attempt at the future unification of the sciences, concepts must be reduced to the same level of analysis if they are to be compared, let alone reconciled.

As with the shards of a mirror, their mere collection cannot create a unified image.

---

57 Richard Rorty (1979).
58 Jacques Derrida (1976).
59 Philipp Frank (1955).

4. Controversy amongst world-views

4.1 The naïve view of the world, the *a priori* philosophy of intuition, is given by biology – a view which changes and develops with the synthesis of new experience and tools of analysis.[60] One moves to reason as one induces and deduces; by interrogating the subjective experience of the world through the establishment of fact.[61] When it is found that reality is other than what it was intuited to be, the authority of reason over the intuition can be denied and beliefs may be persisted with regardless – even to the detriment of those who hold such beliefs.[62] The acquisition of knowledge, or the faculty of reason, can only be achieved by the conformity of our minds to fact.

4.2 How the world is is a matter of conjecture, but the world is. The very existence of any individual implies the existence of the rest of the universe as a closed, and interdependent, system. Physics, our symbolic representation of reality,[63] is an adequate system of reality.[64] The individual, as a physical entity, is proof that the world exists by necessity. At the same time conceptual entities, like those of mathematics, are events in the mind and are limited by the world of logic.[65] But concepts themselves, since they are from the mind, are also of the individual thus physical phenomena. If the individual exists, the world must exist necessarily.

---

60 Barry Smith & Roberto Casati (1994).
61 William Whewell (1860).
62 Daniel Goleman (1985).
63 Albert Einstein (1922): "As far as the laws of mathematics refer to reality, they are not certain; and as far as they are certain, they do not refer to reality".
64 Physics is sufficient to model the world. But when we say that physics is complete, we mean that the physical world is a closed and complete system. Physics itself cannot claim completeness as it is not an exact theory of reality. It is just a model of the closed and complete system. See David Spurrett (1999).
65 Lilianne Kfia (1993).

To question the existence of the world is as dubious as questioning the existence of self. Because, what is self? Self is accomplished through the world – self is a product of the world.

4.3 To question whether or not an individual can interact with another individual in any meaningful way is contradictory. Private language, namely the purely subjective symbolism expressing one's own experience, refers to a state of affairs that is objective. No matter the code of the private language, it does not bar communication because the private language is decipherable by accessing its grammar.[66] The difference in reference means only that something is described from a different perspective. It is only satisfied by particular meanings irrespective of the perspective of the individual, although denoted or signified within his private language.[67]

Individuals attempting communication could be using the same words for concepts, but non-congruently; understanding the meanings of the words differently. Individuals attach particular meanings to terms which show their respective ability to effectively discriminate between meanings. Despite non-congruency in the employment of terms, the correspondence of meanings allows communication to take place.

Superficially communication purports to function on the names things are given (their denotation) contrary to the fact that communication does not work on the names things are

---

66 Denoting, the creation of symbolic expressions, is common to all individuals, even if their expressions of it differ. To know if another individual has a toothache (an expression from the biological language system), or if the individual expresses the same concept in words (namely, that from the learnt language system), is deduced from their grammar – i.e., the rules regulating the use of expressions that we read as meanings about particular things.

67 Ludwig Wittgenstein (1974). See also Cora Diamond (2000).

given, but on what meanings are attributed to these names which represent some thing.[68]

4.4 If incommensurability is the case in empirical matters, then perceptual agnosticism is implied. If physical observations cannot be compared, then conclusions about them cannot be drawn. Without grounds for comparison, namely a common context, no facts can be established and ideas about the physical world cannot be communicated. Biology is the foundation of all conceptual frameworks and it is thereby that observation is theory-laden,[69] and not necessarily theory laden only through the influence of the prevailing paradigm. Theories may be historically incomparable but are not incommensurable in the formal sense.[70] Since biology is reasonably common across all people, there are always grounds for comparative reasoning or perspective analysis.

4.5 It is true that the absence of evidence is not the evidence of absence (i.e., as a counter example); but the evidence of absence is evidence of falsity in each and every case.[71] Scepticism is a matter of probability, and not truly an agnostic belief.[72] One need not be certain of the truth-functional validity of a statement in order to act upon it. That is to say that all matters are in the scope of the theory of probability,[73] as is meaning in communication.

---

68 The superficial view is intuited because it is the very name of things from which we assume, rightly or wrongly, what meanings have been attributed to them.
69 Paul Churchland (1991).
70 Thomas Kuhn (1962). See also Carl Kordig (1971).
71 Karl Popper (1959).
72 All sceptics are unified in the belief that nothing is certain. They are divided by what this entails: the scepticism of antiquity was one of agnostic belief (namely, a complete unknowing), whereas the modern conception is of uncertainty. The antiquated use of scepticism is derived from the false dichotomy between gnosticism (knowing or absolute knowledge) and agnosticism (absolute unknowing). See William Guthrie (1950) and David Hume (1748).
73 Ernest Nagel (1955).

5.   Understanding as knowledge

5.1 As understanding is knowing – knowing how to do something, the ability to respond appropriately to a given situation or stimulus – the faculty of understanding is redundant. If the effective execution of a program or giving an appropriate response to a situation is not manifest of understanding, what, then, would it be to understand? Is the manifestation of understanding not a behaviour, a demonstration of knowing?[74]

The faculty of understanding as something separate to a physical phenomenon (e.g., separate from a brain-state) is a metaphysical notion.[75] The current conception implies a link with the indefinitive functions of consciousness in the sense of mind (as opposed to the body or brain). But we need not 'understand' persons in the same way we need not 'understand' rocks or fruit: we need only know the expressions of the changes in their state, within their environment, which are what define them.[76] We know them through abstraction based on observation of their states. If we call such a process understanding then we have a different kind of concept to the metaphysical notion of knowing and understanding; one that establishes the relationship between knowledge and understanding as an empirical one.[77]

---

74   John Searle (1980).
75   David Chalmers (1996).
76   Communication processes have their own contexts or levels of sophistication, and that there are expressions to be found in all ecological systems is not to say that every entity communicates as persons do.
77   In other words, knowledge is the effective employment of information within a context, thus an understanding of some thing. Information is just the available expressions for analysis, so information is not knowledge nor is it necessarily related to understanding (although understanding is necessarily related to information and expression).

5.2 Accurate communicative effectiveness (understanding the message of a communication) is the arousal of specific meanings through the exchange of any particular symbols. These symbols do not have to be replicated, so long as there is correspondence in meaning. For example, the communication of a meaning may not necessarily be through the use of the same symbol so long as its use stimulates the desired belief or response. When we speak of understanding, we speak of the effective reception of codes resulting in appropriate responses to information or stimulus.

Understanding, itself, can only be within a context. To have an effective exchange of codes (symbols) is to understand something within a particular discourse. That particular use of expression may be utterly inappropriate outside that particular discourse, so the effective use of codes in one discourse does not entail understanding in any other context.[78] Other levels of understanding, namely the code of a particular discourse or context, would have to be learnt in order that it may also be understood and its code used effectively.

---

78 The effective use of statements in one discourse does not entail the propriety of its statements in any other. Statements cannot be taken from higher or lower levels of discourse to be of direct sensibility within another discourse. Although the meanings of lower levels are presumed in the higher levels in that the lower levels are constituent of the higher levels, those meanings are irreducible within the discourse in question. See also Lev Vygotsky (1962).

6. Problems of translation and transposition

6.1 Words, by their very nature, are fickle. It is the context (the way in which they are used in a particular milieu) that sets the scope, defines the linguistic limits. This is particularly true when translating from one language to another. Often what is seen as a non-translatable phrase is the result of a lacuna, or lexical gap.[79]

All that is necessary is that the language must have, or can readily develop, the conceptual platform and vocabulary to express the term or proposition in need of translation.[80] But the meaning of a translation cannot be surely known for what it actually means.[81] For example, Quine hypothesises about someone trying to establish the meaning of utterances from a native people. A rabbit is pointed out and the word *"gavagai"* is spoken. This individual, suggests Quine, would not know what *"gavagai"* really means – whether it means 'undetached rabbit part' or just 'rabbit'.[82] But no-one could actually know what *"gavagai"* means. From the same empirical poverty which the individual would suffer in the translational indeterminacy of a foreign term is that which the native speaker would suffer in the learning process of the word during the acquisition of the language.

6.2 A translation is bound to inaccuracy if it has not captured the idiom or the *zeitgeist* of a text which is an element contained in the cultural context of the language. Thus, in translation, the problem of identifying the context and intent is amplified

---

79   Igor Panasiuk (2005).

80   Giles Gray & Claude Wise (1959): "Whenever human experience enlarges, symbolic expressions are soon found for the new experience, if it is to be treated ideationally at all."

81   That is because words do not have any *actual* meaning (apart from our attribution of meanings to them).

82   Willard Quine (1970).

because there is no way to test the validity of a statement unless both languages are understood within their conventions. That is to say that there are no grounds of comparison between the two without the prior familiarity and understanding of both. They must be brought to equivalent planes in order that they be transposed. But the learnt language system is not static or *a priori*, so conclusiveness will always be lacking.

The problem of translation and transposition can be illustrated by translating an unambiguous sentence from English to becoming equivocal in *isiZulu*. The phrase "This meat is raw" translates to "*Lenyama ihlaza*". The translated phrase is ambiguous without further contextualization within *isiZulu* as the phrase could mean that the meat is raw, that it is green, or that it is blue, or even rude. Even when the sentence is phrased in such a way to identify a property of the subject, e.g., "The greenness of the meat", which translates to "*ubuhlaza benyama*" which means 'the greenness/ blueness/ rawness/ rudeness of the meat', it is still ambiguous. There are discriminatory phrases that are to separate these instances such as saying "*lenyama inobuhlaza besibakabaka*" meaning 'this meat has the green/ blue/ rawness/ rudeness of the sky' to which reason dictates only the meaning 'blue' to be correct; or "*lenyama inobuhlaza botshani*" meaning 'this meat has the green/ blue/ rawness/ rudeness of grass' to which the context of the language again limits the truth possibility of the phrase down to what is logically consistent. The truth of the third instance can be given by the use of negation or an explanatory phrase of the like (e.g. 'the meat you are *cooking*, or have cooked, is *raw*' that translates to "*lenyama* **oyiphekayo**, *noma oyiphekhile*, **ihlaza**". That the meat is rude is always ambiguous, or even illegitimate, as no possible instance of it can be given.[83]

---

83 It is an anthropomorphic fallacy.

6.3 Truth predicates in a sentence apply to elements within a sentence,[84] but the veracity of truth is about the sentence and is not contained within the actual sentence.[85] It is true that the statement 'It is true that Lunga is a good tennis coach' is equivalent to "Lunga is a good tennis coach", but the veracity of truth is actually dependant on whether or not the predication or notion of truth reflects reality (i.e: whether or not there is a 'Lunga', that this Lunga coaches tennis, and that Lunga is *really* a good tennis coach).

The notion of predication of truth, within the context of a sentence, is usually what is put to question. Its veracity, however, must be tested by actuality. Veracity is strictly empirical.

---

84 Alfred Ayer (1946): "There are sentences... in which the word "truth" seems to stand for something real; and this leads the speculative philosopher to enquire what this "something" is. Naturally he fails to obtain a satisfactory answer, since his question is illegitimate."
85 Alfred Tarski (1933).

7. Relations amongst complex sentences

7.1 Statements or the reference to a class of statements, namely statements that are generalizations of instances of other statements, are in the domain of an object-language for those instances. The status of those instances or the status of their generalizations – i.e.: the truth-functional validity of those statements – are propositions of their metalanguage (namely, metastatements). That is just but another way of saying that the content of the refined context is contained within the greater context of the subject; and that this greater context encompasses all statements of the refined context including statements about their status.

The content and its subject of the refined context has its analogue as the object-language; the greater context encompassing all the meanings of the refined context and their validity is analogous to the metalanguage.

For example: if we have a language for talking about women or define women as the subject of our discourse, our context of appropriate meanings is that containing those meanings which are necessary to the subject 'women'. We can call this discourse or domain C_w. If we then wish to speak about a particular type or class of woman, a further restriction is imposed on meanings contained within the context which refines the context to only those meanings that are about that class or particular type of woman. We can denote this as C_{w-1}.[86] C_w is then the metalanguage for C_{w-1}, and C_{w-1} is the object-language for C_w in terms of C_w.

---

86 The subscripts 'w-1' and, later, 'w+1' are used for the convenience of this example, and are used in this way to illustrate, as clearly as possible, the differences in complexity (i.e., order) between inclusive contexts.

If we choose, rather, to discuss the class or type that the subject 'women' is a part of, that discourse encompassing the discourse 'women' and the status of it can be denoted by C_{w+1}. This means that C_{w+1} is the metalanguage for C_w, and C_w is an object-language in terms of C_{w+1}. But C_w is also a metalanguage in terms of C_{w-1}, whereas C_{w-1} is the object-language for C_w and is, thus, also an object language for C_{w+1}. That is to say that C_{w+1} is a metalanguage for both C_w and C_{w-1}.

The relationship between metalanguage and object-language is relative to the definition of the refined context. And vice versa, depending on whether the object-language or the metalanguage is taken as the basis of discourse.[87]

7.2 Establishing, or ascertaining, equivalent planes of analysis for properly evaluating content is the essential function of context. To elaborate on this point, one can use the Liar's Paradox:

(i) This statement is false.

Statement (i) is the metastatement of some other subordinate statement; namely, that which the phrase 'this statement' refers to. It is legitimate to ask of (i) 'which statement?' so that the instance which it refers to may be checked to see if it is true or false, in order to attain the truth-functional validity of (i). Therefore (i) is either true or false, and exclusively so.

If the answer to the question 'which statement?' is self-referential – in other words, the validity of 'this statement is false' must be ascertained without reference to any other statement other than (i) – then we are dealing with only the

---

87   Rudolf Carnap (1955).

status of (i) which is, in fact, the metastatement for (i). That is to say that if (i) is self-referential, namely the object-language for the metastatement (i), we are not dealing with any other postulates than the postulate of whether or not it is valid or even legitimate to state (i).

If the statement is self-referential then the phrase 'this statement' is void of meaning as a generalization because it has no instances to justify its place within the context (i.e., it is circular). If the statement (i) is to have a conclusive meaning, it must be in reference to an instance outside of self-reference. So whether or not (i) is valid is dependent on the meaning attributed to it within the metalanguage. But since the meaning of (i) and 'this statement' are components of the metalanguage for (i), (i) is undecidably true or false until an instance or meaning for 'this statement' is given within the object-language for (i). It still holds, then, that (i) is either true or false exclusively.[88]

---

88 Otherwise we end up with an infinite regression of 'this statement' without reference to anything other than 'this statement' and so on, *ad infinitum.*

8. The necessity for the full disclosure of information

8.1 The problem is often that of asking the correct questions as opposed to the methods in which the answer is given (although the method in which the answer is given is obviously essential). With a poorly formed question, the answer is bound to suffer the same deficits as the question. A more astute question, on the other hand, calls for full disclosure of the facts of the matter. For instance, in situations where the statement is not ambiguous and contains all the relevant relations, it provides a full disclosure of the information asked. The question or statement need not be polar (either the one or the other), but the same principle of relation applies with each additional element.

8.2 Bias results from axioms which are the context that is set. Axioms, statements of 'givens', are the foundations of a particular language system, and any expression produced outside of their discourse is indecipherable and ungrammatical within that discourse. These expressions are formally undecidable as their actuality cannot be proved the one way or the other within that particular context.[89]

8.3 The grammar of a valid argument must: (1) have all its elements related by an explicit criterion of characteristics, and (2) must be formulated to explore the truth-functional value of its elements according to such criteria. Any argument or set of propositions intended as a formula that does not meet this grammar is illegitimate.

---

89   Alfred Tarski (1956); Kurt Gödel (1963). See also Martin Davis (1958) and Roman Murawski (1998).

9. The role of authority

9.1 We have an inherent bias towards authority because of the improbability of an arbitrary individual outside of a specialised field stumbling upon a significant insight. Nonetheless, the appeal to authority may be fallacious as an irrelevant appeal to authority in support of an argument (or, conversely, the dismissal of an argument on the grounds that it lacks authoritative approval), viz.: *argumentum ad verecundiam.*

BIBLIOGRAPHY

Ayer, Alfred. *Language, truth and logic* (London: Gollancz, 2nd Edition, 1946).

Ayer, Alfred. *The foundations of empirical knowledge* (London: Macmillan, 1940).

Carnap, Rudolf. *The Logical Syntax of Language* (London: Routledge & Kegan Paul, 1937).

Carnap, Rudolf. Foundations of logic and mathematics. In: Otto Neurath, Rudolf Carnap & Charles Morris (eds), *International Encyclopedia of Unified Science* 1(1):141-214 (University of Chicago Press, 1955).

Carnap, Rudolf. 24. Elementary and abstract terms. Foundations of logic and mathematics. In: Otto Neurath, Rudolf Carnap & Charles Morris (eds), *International Encyclopedia of Unified Science* 1(1):203-209 (University of Chicago Press, 1955).

Carnap, Rudolf. Intellectual autobiography. In: Schilpp, P. A. (ed.), *The Philosophy of Rudolf Carnap* XI (LaSalle, Illinois: Open Court, 1963).

Cantor, Paul. The Scientist and the Poet. *The New Atlantis*, **4**: 75-85 (2004).

Chalmers, David. *The Conscious Mind* (Oxford University Press: 1996).

Chomsky, Noam. *Language and problems of knowledge: the Managua lectures* (MIT Press, 1987).

Chomsky, Noam. On the nature, use, and acquisition of language. In: W.C. Ritchie & T.K. Bhatia (eds) *Handbook of Child Language Acquisition* (San Diego: Academic Press, 1999).

Christiansen, Morten & Nick Chater. Language as shaped by the brain. In: *Behavioural and brain sciences* (Cambridge University Press, 2008).

Churchland, Paul. A deeper unity: Some Feyerabendian themes in neurocomputational form. In: G. Munevar (ed.), *Beyond reason: Essays on the philosophy of Paul Feyerabend*, pp.1-23 (Boston: Kluwer Academic Publishers, 1991). Reprinted in: R. N. Giere (ed.), Cognitive models of science, *Minnesota Studies in the Philosophy of Science XV* (1992).

Croce, Benedetto. *Breviario di estetica* (1913). *The essence of aesthetic* (translated by Douglas Ainslie) (London: William Heinemann, 1921).

Davis, Martin. *Computability and unsolvability* (McGraw-Hill Education, 1958).

Deleuze, Gilles. *Difference and repetition* (1968) (translated by Paul Patton) (New York: Columbia University Press, 1994).

Derrida, Jacques. *De la grammatologie* (Les Éditions de Minuit, 1967). *Of grammatology* (translated by Gayatri Chakravorty Spivak) (Johns Hopkins University Press, 1976, corrected edition, 1998).

Devlin, Keith. Situation Theory and Situation Semantics. In: *Handbook of the History of Logic* (Elsevier, 2006).

Dewey, John. The relation of science and philosophy as the basis of education. *School and Society* **47** (9 April 1938). Reprinted in: *Philosophy of Education (Problems of Men)* (Ames, Iowa: Littlefield Adams, 1956).

Dewhurst, Tessa. The epistemology of testimony: Fulfilling the sincerity condition. *South African Journal of Philosophy* (2009).

Dewhurst, Therese. *Take my word for it: A new approach to the problem of sincerity in the epistemology of testimony.* (M.Phil Thesis, Rhodes University, 2010).

Diamond, Cora. Does Bismark have a beetle in his box? The private language argument in the *Tractatus*. In: Alice Crary and Rupert Read (eds), *The new Wittgenstein* (London: Routledge, 2000).

Donne, John. Now, this bell tolling softly for another, says to me: Thou must die. *Devotions upon emergent Occasions,* Meditation XVII *Nunc lento sonitu dicunt, morieris* (London: Thomas Jones, 1624).

Eco, Umberto. *A theory of semiotics* (Indiana University Press, 1976).

Einstein, Albert. I. Geometry and experience. In: *Sidelights on relativity* (London: Methuen, 1922).

Feferman, Solomon. 1. Deciding the undecidable: Wrestling with Hilbert's problems. In: *In the light of logic* (New York: Oxford University Press, 1998).

Foucault, Michel. Theatrum philosophicum [book review of Deleuze, G., *Différence et répétition* (1969) and *Logique du sens* (1969)] *Critique* no. 282: 885-908 (November 1970).

Frank, Philipp. Foundations of physics. In: Otto Neurath, Rudolf Carnap & Charles Morris (eds), *International Encyclopedia of Unified Science* **1**(2):427-504 (University of Chicago Press, 1955).

Frege, Gottlob. Über Sinn und Bedeutung, *Zeitschrift für Philosophie und philosophische Kritik* **100**: 25-50 (1892). *On sense and reference* (translated by Max Black). In Geach, P. and Black, M. (eds) *Translations from the philosophical writings of Gottlob Frege* (Blackwell, 1952, 2nd edition 1960).

Frege, Gottlob. *Begriffsschrift eine der arithmetischen nachgebildete Formelsprache des reinen Denkens* (Halle: Louis Nebert, 1879). *Begriffsschrift, a formula language, modelled upon that of arithmetic, for pure thought* translated by S. Bauer-Mengelberg. In: Jean Van Heijenoort (ed.) *From Frege to Gödel: A Source Book in Mathematical Logic*, 1879–1931 (Harvard University Press, 1967).

Gödel, Kurt. "Über formal unentscheidbare Sätze der Principia Mathematica und verwandter Systeme I" *Monatshefte für Mathematik und Physic*, 38: 173- 198 (1931) [paper dated 17 November 1930]. *On formally undecidable propositions of principia mathematica and related systems I* translated by Bernard Meltzer (Basic Books, 1963).

Goleman, Daniel. *Vital lies, simple truths: the psychology of self-deception* (New York: Simon & Schuster, 1985).

Gray, Giles & Claude Wise. *The bases of speech* (New York: Harper, 1934, 3rd edition, 1959).

Guthrie, William. *The Greek philosophers from Thales to Aristotle* (London: Methuen, 1950).

Hardt, Michael and Antonio Negri. *Empire* (Cambridge, Massachussetts: Harvard University Press, 2000).

Hilbert, David. Mathematical problems. *Bulletin of the American Mathematical Society* **8**:437-479 (1902).

Hofstadter, Douglas. *Gödel, Escher, Bach: An eternal golden braid* (Basic Books, 1979, 20th anniversary edition, 1999).

Hrehor, Kristin. *Recognition and reconciliation: The new role of theory in aesthetics* (Master's Thesis, Queen's University, 2007).

Hume, David. *A treatise of treatise of human nature: Being an attempt to introduce the experimental method of reasoning into moral subjects* (London: John Noon, 1739).

Hume, David. *An Enquiry concerning Human Understanding* (1748).

Ingarden, Roman. *Spór o istnienie świata* (PAU, Vol. I, Kraków: 1947, Vol. II, Kraków, 1948).*Time and Modes of Being* (translated by Helen R. Michejda) (Springfield, Illinois: Charles C. Thomas, 1964).

Joseph, Rhawn. The limbic system. *Neuropsychiatry, Neuropsychology, Clinical Neuroscience* (New York: Academic Press, 2000).

Kfia, Lilianne (Mujica-Parodi). The ontological status of mathematical entities: the necessity for modern physics of a re-evaluation of mathematical systems. *Review of Metaphysics* **47**(1):19-42 (1993).

Kruger, Justin & David Dunning. Unskilled and unaware of it: How difficulties in recognizing one's own incompetence lead to inflated self-assessments. *Journal of Personality and Social Psychology* **77**(6): 121-1134 (1999).

Kordig, Carl. The comparability of scientific theories. *Philosophy of Science* **38**(4): 467-485 (1971).

Kuhn, Thomas. *The structure of scientific revolutions* (Chicago: University of Chicago Press, 1962).

Locke, John. *An essay concerning human understanding* (1690).

Malthus, Thomas. *An essay on the principle of population, or, A view of its past and present effects on human happiness, with an inquiry into our prospects respecting the future removal or mitigation of the evils which it occasions* (1st edition 1798, 6th edition revised by the author 1826).

Mayr, Ernst. Teleological and teleonomic, a new analysis. *Boston Studies in the Philosophy of Science* **14**: 91-117 (1974).

Maslow, Abraham. A theory of human motivation. *Psychological Review* **50**: 370-396 (1943).

Morgan, Edwin. *The Second Life* (Edinburgh University Press, 1968).

Murawski, Roman. Undefinability of truth. The problem of the priority: Tarski Vs. Gödel. *History and Philosophy of Logic* **19**:153-160 (1998).

Nagel, Ernest. Principles of the theory of probability. In: Otto Neurath, Rudolf Carnap & Charles Morris (eds), *International Encyclopedia of Unified Science* **1**(2):343-422 (University of Chicago Press, 1955).

Newman, John. The Mission of St. Benedict. *Atlantis of January* (Oxford: 1858.)

Panasiuk, Igor. Kulturelle Aspekte der Übersetzung: Anwendung des ethnopsycholinguistischen Lakunen-Modells auf die Analyse und Übersetzung literarischer Texte (Lit, Münster, 2005).

Peacock, Thomas. The four ages of poetry. *Olliers literary miscellany in prose and verse by several hands to be continued occasionally*, **1**: 183-200 (London: Charles Ollier, 1820).

Peirce, Charles. Questions concerning certain faculties claimed for man. *Journal of Speculative Philosophy* **2**: 103-114 (1868).

Popper, Karl. *The logic of scientific discovery* (translation of *Logik der Forschung*, Vienna, 1935) (London: Hutchinson, 1959).

Putnam, Hilary. *The threefold cord: mind, body, and world* (New York: Columbia University Press, 1999).

Quine, Willard. Two Dogmas of Empiricism. *The Philosophical Review* **60**: 20-43, (1951). Reprinted in: Willard Quine, *From a Logical Point of View* (Harvard University Press, 1953).

Quine, Willard. *Ontological relativity and other essays* (Columbia University Press, New York, 1970).

Ramose, Mogobe. The struggle for reason in Africa. In: Coetzee, P.H. & Roux, A.P.J. (eds), [Introduction to] *The African philosophy reader* (New York: Routledge, 2003).

Rorty, Richard. *Philosophy and the Mirror of Nature* (USA: Princeton University Press, 1979).

Russell, Bertrand. *The principles of mathematics* (Cambridge University Press, 1903).

Russell, Bertrand. *The problems of philosophy* (London: Oxford University Press, 1912).

Russell, Bertrand. *Theory of knowledge: The 1913 manuscript.* Elizabeth R. Eames & Kenneth Blackwell (eds) (London: George Allen & Unwin, 1984).

Sartre, Jean-Paul. *Question de méthode* (1958). *The Search for Method* (translated by Hazel Barnes) (New York: Random House, Vintage Books, 1968).

Saussure, Ferdinand de. *Course in General Linguistics* (Translated from the original 1916 French edition by Wade Baskin) (New York: Philosophical Library, 1959).

Schopenhauer, Arthur. The art of literature: Essay 1 - On authorship. From *The essays of Arthur Schopenhauer* (translated by Thomas Bailey Saunders) (1891) from *Parerga und Paralipomena* (1851).

Searle, John. Minds, brains, and programs. *Behavioural and Brain Sciences* **3**(3): 417-457 (1980).

Shelley, Percy. A defence of poetry. *Essays, Letters from Abroad, Translations and Fragments* (London: Edward Moxon, 1840).

Shute, Nevil. *Pastoral* (New York: William Morrow, 1944).

Smith, Barry & Roberto Casati. Naïve physics: An essay in ontology. *Philosophical Psychology*, **7**(2): 225-244 (1994).

Spurrett, David. *The completeness of physics* (D.Phil. thesis, University of Natal, 1999).

Tarski, Alfred. *Pojęcie prawdy w językach nauk dedukcyjnych* (1933). *Logic, semantics, metamathematics* (Translation by Alfred Tarski) (Oxford Clarendon Press, 1956).

Tarski, Alfred. The semantic conception of truth and the foundations of semantics. *Philosophy and phenomenonological research* **4**: 341-376 (1944).

Tubbs, Stewart & Sylvia Moss. *Human communication.* (5th edition, Random House, 1987).

Vygotsky, Lev. *Thought and language* (translated by Eugenia Hanfmann and Gertrude Vakar) (Cambridge: M.I.T. Press, 1962).

Vyshedskiy, Andrey. *On the origin of the human mind* (Canada: MobileReference, 2008).

Whewell, William. *On the philosophy of discovery* (London, 1860).

Whorf, Benjamin Lee. The relation of habitual thought and behaviour to language. In: Leslie Spier (ed.) *Language, culture, and personality, essays in memory of Edward Sapir,* pp 75-93 (Menasha, Wisconsin: Sapir Memorial Publication Fund, 1941).

Wimsatt, William & Monroe Beardsley. The affective fallacy. *Sewanee Review* **57**(1): 31-55 (1949).

Wittgenstein, Ludwig. Logisch-Philosophische Abhandlung. *Annalen der Naturphilosophie* (1921). *Tractatus Logico-Philosophicus* (translated by Charles K. Ogden [assisted by Frank Ramsey]) (London: Kegan Paul, 1922) and later translation by David Pears and Brian McGuinness (London: Routledge & Kegan Paul, 1961, revised edition 1974).

Wittgenstein, Ludwig. *Philosophical investigations* (translated by Gertrude E. M. Anscombe) (Oxford: Basil Blackwell, 1974).

Other cited resources:

Graphic Images (paintings, drawings, photographs)

Magritte, René. *The treachery of images,* 1929 (painting, 1928-1929).
Escher, Maurits. *Drawing hands* (lithograph, 1968).
Joyner, Eric. *Tin robots, submerged* (image, 2009).

Miscellaneous

Shakur, Tupac. *Mama's just a little girl,* Better Dayz disc one (Interscope Records, 2002).

* * * * *

A word of respect and appreciation is due to open internet resource sites like Google and Scribd, without whom research would have been a more cumbersome task. Accessibility and open access to information promotes progress, so I applaud and give my support to the endeavour. ~ P.M.M.

Printed in the United States
by Baker & Taylor Publisher Services